The Transformation of Suffering

The Transformation
of Suffering

Reflections on September 11 & the Wedding Feast at Cana in Galilee

Thomas Keating

Lantern Books ● New York
A Division of Booklight Inc.

2002
Lantern Books
One Union Square West, Suite 201
New York, NY 10003

Scripture texts taken from The New Testament translated by James A. Kleist, SJ, and Joseph L. Lilly GM, Bruce Publishing Co, Milwaukee, 1956, except Wedding Feast of Cana (John 2:1–11) © Confraternity of Christian Doctrine, Washington, D.C., 1970 as it appears·in The Vatican II Sunday Missal.

Printed in the United States of America

Library of Congress Cataloging-in-Publication Data

Keating, Thomas.
  The transformation of suffering : reflections on September 11 and the marriage feast at Cana of Galilee / by Thomas Keating.
      p. cm.
   ISBN 1-59056-036-1
  1. September 11 Terrorist Attacks, 2001. 2. Suffering—Religious aspects—Catholic Church. 3. Turning water into wine at the wedding at Cana (Miracle) I. Title.
   BT732.7 .K43 2002
   248.8'6—dc21

                                        2002006012

❈ *Contents* ❈

❈ *Part One* ❈

*A Christian Perspective
on September 11, 2001*

I HAPPENED TO be in New York at the time of the tragedy of September 11, 2001 and felt the groundswell of grief, anguish, and indignation that rolled over the city and far afield. I found in other parts of the world where I went soon afterward a great sympathy for the United States, and a similar concern for the world. It became clearer after that day that this attack was basically an attack on humanity, not just New York or the United States. Indeed, there were, according to some estimates, eighty different nationalities represented in the towers at the time of their destruction.

As I watched the terrible scene on the television, I had no immediate reaction. As the days passed on, I realized that at first no particular reaction was possible for me because of the overwhelming grief that pervaded every other reaction.

In the days immediately following September 11, a lot of people were in a state of shock. That state of shock may well continue for many persons as the psychological effects of it gradually unfold over the months and years to come. We have little idea of all the ramifications of such a major event.

What struck me most was the visible character of the event. This was a culmination of a whole series of other tragic, violent, and brutalizing events that have been building up over the past eighty to one hundred years. These may have been equally shocking events for the human family. But in previous times, we were not aware of them to the degree that we are vulnerable to such tragedies now. Modern technology—television, radio, the Internet, cellular phones—makes them instantaneously available. I would hazard a guess that this event was seen by most of the people in the world.

What also seemed to me significant as I reflected on the event was that, at least since the First World War, there has been an ever-increasing disregard for innocent people in violent situations—especially wars. Indeed, we might say that at least from the middle of the twentieth century it is safer in wartime to be in the military rather than to be a civilian. The equation between those killed in combat and those killed as a consequence of military action has become much more weighted on the side of the men, women, and children who happen to get in the way. This new kind of war is called total war, meaning that everybody living in a country under attack, however innocent, or even opposed to the actions of its government, is considered an enemy.

Christ's Crucifixion

September 11 was a visible tragedy. I can think of other terrible tragedies, much more devastating in terms of the numbers of deaths than the destruction of the Twin Towers: the Holocaust, the Gulag, the two world wars, Rwanda, Cambodia, Vietnam, the cultural revolution in China, and the AIDS epidemic. All these horrors reached a climax on a gorgeous September day in New York with the unbelievable events we saw on the television in front of our eyes.

We were acutely aware of the people in the building. While there were close to three thousand deaths, it is worth remembering that thirty to forty thousand people worked in the two buildings. It was almost miraculous that so many people actually got out alive. Perhaps the prayers of those who were looking at the collapse of the towers on the television or heard of it on the radio contributed to their escape.

In any case, what I saw, and it is only my vision of it, was an image of the crucifixion of Christ, extended to the whole of humanity. The two towers, for me, were like the two arms of Christ on the cross, reaching up to heaven for mercy and to all appearances receiving no answer. The scene in lower Manhattan was the crucifixion of humanity, so to speak, extended in this enormous, visible, and public way—surely one of the most extraordinary signs of all time. As a consequence, its universal character, as seen by everybody in the world, must be a message to humanity of the most profound kind, especially if we can begin to fathom it by prayer and not be carried away by grief, anger, and retaliatory emotions.

The Unity of the Human Family

There is no doubt in my mind that we are in an extraordinary period in which the most basic values of humanity are being challenged and are at stake. In addition, our personal relationship to those values is being challenged.

Just as there has been a gradual buildup of horror and terror through the wars and human tragedies I mentioned above, so there has been an increasing attack on the human family. The attack on the Twin Towers is a deliberate rejection of the oneness of the human family that the gospel and most other religions proclaim.

The human family is essentially a single species. In fact, biophysics, quantum mechanics, and other contemporary sciences are now affirming that everything in the cosmos is interconnected and interrelated, especially all life forms.

The basic structure of the universe, the stars and planets, the possibility of life—the very possibility of our being here at this moment—were all present in the first trillionth of a trillionth of a trillionth of a second that can now, so science tells us, be calibrated. Scientists explain that the material that came into existence at the moment of the Big Bang was so incredibly dense that the force that spread it apart and allowed the universe to expand must have required inconceivable power. Nobody has an explanation for what force blew apart the original energy when it was all in one place, in a size so tiny that it boggles the imagination.

Just as it is hard to conceive of the beginnings of the universe, it is equally hard to grasp that everything—from the smallest subatomic particle to us human beings—emerged by stages from that source. We are thus embedded in the structure of the universe. All life, moreover, contains the same basic cells—so much so that there is little cellular difference between a mouse and us. There is even less difference among us as human beings. Contemporary science reinforces the biblical claim that the human family was made out of the dust of the earth. The Book of Genesis and the gospels emphasize the unity of the human family.

Just how deep this unity actually is is still to be grasped by most of us. For one thing, it would not have been possible for Christ to take the whole human family into himself, as we Christians believe he did in the Incarnation, unless the human species itself was integrally one. Only in this way could Christ, by taking one human nature to himself, take to himself the nature of everybody—with every-body's personal history, suffering, joys, and failures.

Christ's identification with the human family as evolving or as fallen, whichever way you prefer to look at it, is central to our Christian faith and to the redemption. If we were not one as a race, Christ could not have died for our sins. And St. Paul teaches that if Christ has not died for our sins, we are still in them.

This understanding of the unity of the human family is central to Christianity. Our spiritual journey, especially contemplative prayer, together with its practices for daily life, are processes of becoming aware of just how profound that unity is—with God, ourselves, other people, other living beings, the earth, and all creation.

We are taught in theology that God is infinite. If God is infinite, there is no room for anything else. In this perspective, everything created remains in God, and God dwells in everything that exists. The omnipresence of God tells us that the most important element of everything, especially of every human being, is not *us*, but the presence of God *in us*.

In the development of our spiritual journey, each of us is invited, as Jesus put it in Matthew 6:6, to enter our inner room. Our inner room is the place of encounter with the Divine Indwelling, with the God who dwells within us. It is the spiritual space where God interacts with us at levels that we do not fully understand but may sometimes intuit. Through contemplative prayer, this relationship deepens and develops into the capacity to perceive God in everything, especially in other people. We begin to see beyond our superficial judgments of others to the reality of the divine presence that underlies everyone's existence, including the people we most dislike and consider our enemies.

Yes. God loves our enemies, too. This thought may make us somewhat uncomfortable at first, but we may as well get used to it. The feelings of retaliation and revenge that we all normally feel to some degree when we have been mistreated are regressions to the primitive level of human reactions. In a crisis, we either go forward with the challenge or, looking desperately for some form of security, sink back into forms of response that were familiar and expressed at earlier periods in our life.

A New Kind of Martyrdom

The people who lost their lives in the Twin Towers on September 11 are not martyrs in the strict sense of the word. They did not die for a cause. But perhaps we can affirm that they pioneered a new kind of martyrdom. They entered into the kind of redemptive suffering that Jesus himself experienced and manifested. They laid down their lives not just for a cause, but, like Jesus, for the whole human family.

These men and women were trying to earn a living in that building. Most of them didn't own the companies that were housed there. Many of them were just ordinary office workers, or people who worked in the restaurants or cleaned the place. The heroic firefighters and police officers who went in to try to rescue them are in a special category.

All of these people have moved into the kind of glory we think of when we talk in terms of martyrdom for religious reasons or for motives of justice. For me, the reason they are martyrs is that the world has moved into a new perspective in which particular causes are not as significant as the continuation of the human family itself. And this is what is being called in question by the terrorist mentality.

I have already catalogued some of the tragedies of the past hundred years. The amount of human suffering in the form of deliberate violence, brutality, torture, and indifference that has been experienced and meted out reaches beyond our ability either to comprehend or to imagine. Along with the exponential increase in the human population, there has been an exponential increase in tragedy and violence. One way of conceiving of such horrors is to understand them as a layer of negativity in the atmosphere, a result of the selfishness, enmity, and oppression of the human family that have been accumulating in the past few centuries or probably from the very beginning.

This accumulation of evil, both individual and social, descended upon the people who happened to be in the Twin Towers on that day. They bore, so to speak, the collective negativity and sins of the world at that moment. This is why, in dying, they are martyrs in a very real sense, and thus entered immediately into the everlasting life promised to those who lay down their lives for the sake of others and for justice and peace. Nor are they the only innocent ones who may be so richly rewarded. Given the growing sense of indifference to innocent suffering, the fruits of this kind of martyrdom may extend to everybody who is caught in the crossfire of violence, injustice, and hatred, wherever these tragedies are taking place in the world.

As we look around and see some of the desperate needs of people—homelessness, exile, prison, destitution, starvation, chronic mental and physical illness—we should also remember that according to the Bible those who suffer these afflictions are God's special favorites. At the same time, to respond to the suffering of the needy in every way that we possibly can rests squarely on our shoulders.

The United States and the World

Let us briefly explore the background to the tragedy of September 11 and how other parts of the world see the United States. All countries, communities, and even churches suffer from the accumulation of what might be termed the false self ("the old self" in St. Paul's terminology). By the false self I mean the self developed in our own likeness rather than in the likeness of God. It is the self-image developed to cope with the emotional trauma of infancy and early childhood. It seeks happiness in terms of the gratification of the instinctual needs of survival and security, affection and esteem, and power and control, and bases its self-worth on cultural conditioning and group identification.

When these emotional programs for happiness or group identifications are frustrated, off go the afflictive emotions of grief, anger, fear, guilt, shame, humiliation, discouragement, and despair, to name only a few. Commentaries increase the intensity of these emotions and plunge us into emotional binges lasting hours, days, weeks, or months, often leading to personal sin to get away from the pain.

Social sins have been increasing in the last few centuries, just because there are more people who are capable of pouring their personal negativity into the atmosphere. The collapse of the Twin Towers is an image of the collective crucifixion of the human family that has been gradually gathering momentum through wars, social upheavals, and the increasing disregard of the innocent.

Consider Rwanda, for example. Most of the people who died and those who killed them were Christians who turned on each other because of ethnic over-identification. Estimates of the number of the dead vary, but as many as a million people, according to some sources, were massacred. When we think of the numbers who died in the Twin Towers, three thousand seems small by comparison. Yet the visibility of what happened on September

11 has brought into focus the enormous horrors that the past hundred years have inflicted on the human family. September 11 warns us that the way we lead our lives has to be profoundly challenged and changed.

One of the reasons for what happened on September 11 is our unwillingness to respond adequately to those in great need. This expresses itself on national levels in governments seeking only their private interests and not the interests of the larger global community. Obviously, governments have the obligation to defend their people against violent attacks. But along with the need for self-defense is the need to remember that resorting to violence has never solved any situation. It always leads to more violence. Therefore, we—or at least and certainly those in authority—find ourselves in an enormous double bind in which we feel called to heal unjust situations for which we bear collective responsibility, and at the same time to protect innocent people from ongoing attacks.

How nations and their citizens are going to resolve this dilemma, as we can see from the response to the September 11 attack, is an enormous challenge. As I traveled in South Africa in the immediate aftermath of September 11, I noticed that most people had huge sympathy for the United States. But I have observed that, as these individuals have continued to see pictures of men, women, and children who are not involved in military campaigns injured by stray bombs, that sympathy is beginning to wither. In addition, fomenting a reaction within the Muslim world against the United States is one of the hazards that our government has to face. To extremists within Islam, the materialist and consumerist culture of the United States, which was represented by the Twin Towers, was something that they had to destroy. They feared that the process of globalization, which up to now has been driven mostly by economic or informational motivation, will undermine their religious culture and moral values.

Another fundamental issue for Islamic extremists is that they do not relate to the concept of the separation of church and state. In many Islamic countries, the real force behind the throne is the clerics. These clerics and their followers do not have much interest in talking to Western politicians. The only people with whom they might be willing to engage in serious dialogue are the spiritual leaders of other major religions. The need for the latter to reach out in genuine dialogue with the spiritual leaders of Islam is urgent. Otherwise, we may find ourselves in a confrontation of cultures that may become very destructive.

These are the narrow political meanings, as far as I see them, of September 11. What we turn to now are the larger global issues. What lessons for the future of the planet have been manifested by the destruction of the Twin Towers?

The first is that we may be reaching a point in history that some anthropologists have called an axial period. This term, invented by the German philosopher Karl Jaspers (1883–1969), refers to a historical period in which there is a paradigm shift in human consciousness that leads to a new set of values or ways of conceiving human existence. Thus, when I say that we may be at the onset of a new an axial age, I focus primarily on the possibility that we may be entering a new level of understanding regarding the oneness of the human family. As a result, the need to establish a new world economy that can distribute the goods of the earth to all its members, much more than has been done

in the past, has become urgent, if not the top prior-
ity of the world community.

Secondly, there is the fact that terrorism on the
global scale is a new kind of war—one that has not
been faced before. The perpetrators of the attack on
the World Trade Center and the Pentagon, without
using any military weapons at all, destroyed buildings that were built to be indestructible and the
symbols of American financial and military domi-
nation. They shook our materialistic culture to the
roots and dented a certain amount of our pride in
the predominance of our financial success and
power. The destruction was accomplished in a couple of hours with a rudimentary knowledge of fly-
ing and some box-cutters. Through this carefully
planned act, the trillions of dollars put into conven-
tional and nuclear weaponry by this nation were
rendered almost laughable, while ordinary objects
that no one would consider weapons were turned
into artifacts of enormous destruction.

I wonder if we in this country have fully com-
prehended the significance of the message of
September 11, if we still hope that bombs can
resolve the problem of terrorism. It is far from clear
whether we have alienated the Muslim world

through our bombing campaign in Afghanistan, even though every effort was made to avoid civilian casualties. The terrorists have a weapon that is virtually irresistible—this is what is so dangerous. These individuals are prepared to lay down their lives in order to destroy us. Against this disposition, there is no defense.

The result of this mindset is that no place is safe, no person is safe. A terrorist attack could happen at any time and any place, wherever we happen to be in the world. This kind of terror does not only affect Americans. All humanity is realizing that we live in a world that is much more hazardous than most of us thought.

It might be argued that the world has always been this way. What has changed is that now, at least in the U.S., we have been forced to confront it in a way that requires a response—in particular, action on our part to right the imbalances between the well-to-do and the impoverished nations of the world.

In addition to this geopolitical situation, a vast number of the world's scientists believe that the current practices of our industrial cultures are using up the world's resources and bringing us to the very brink of an ecological crisis that may make it impossible for many forms of life to continue to exist on earth. The vitally important issues of resource consumption and global warming have slipped into the background in the face of the terrorist crisis. In any case, for the past several decades many outstanding scientists have been saying that we cannot continue to pollute the oceans, the forests, and the atmosphere without endangering the survival of life itself on the planet.

Thus, two major events are occurring together at this moment of history—and have been, as it were, focused by the Twin Towers disaster—to invite us to reevaluate the way we live and the way we respond to people living in other parts of the world. A kind of midlife crisis has come upon us, and we are questioning the values of the things we thought were important and worth living for before September 11.

The Division and Unity of Religions

This axial age calls into question the needless divisions between Christians and the age-old animosity between the world's religions. The world's religions are the very sources that most promote human values, and yet throughout history the greatest violence has often been perpetrated in the name of religion. This is not primarily the fault of religions but of the fact that religion is one of the aspects of life that gives our primal need for security its greatest support and encouragement. Thus we may find ourselves defending our religion not so much because we regard it as true, but because we require it to bolster our fragile sense of security. Religion speaks to this need with perhaps the strongest voice of any support system in the world. This, I believe, is not true religious expression but a way of using religion as a crutch to shore up our dependency on powerful security symbols.

My particular theory—and it is only a hypoth-esis—is that our moment in history is part of a much larger movement. We might even call it a cos-mic movement, in which, having achieved the great accomplishment of reaching the rational level of consciousness, we are being challenged to move to yet another level of consciousness. This higher level is one that will generalize throughout the con-sciousness of the human family the intuition of the oneness of all that is. It will enable the collective suffering of the human family to find its meaning in contributing a new and in-depth understanding of life to future generations. It will also provide a more realistic and honest relationship with ourselves, God, other people, the planet Earth, and all creation.

In Christian terms, this new moment of history is an invitation to enter into the passion, death, and resurrection of Christ. Although the violence in the world seems to have increased in recent centuries, this violence is not meaningless or worthless. It may be the necessary preparation for a change of consciousness leading to a new level of maturity in the human family as a whole—attitudes that will lead to a much greater concern for every member of the race, past, present, and to come.

This intuition has appeared in the writings of the mystics of our Christian faith as well as in other religions. Christ enters into oneness with us not only as a species but one by one, so that each of us is a unique manifestation of the great love of the Father for humankind. It is a love that goes as far as to send into the human situation—with all of its struggles and failures—the Son of his bosom in order to prove his determination to transform the human family into the divine life, and to grant to all its members the maximum communication of the divine love, truth, and happiness.

This is the contemplative view of the situation in which we find ourselves, one drawn from the mysteries of our Christian faith. It is a view that is also reflected in the other great religions of the world. What these religious expressions have in common is a sense that the human family as a whole has not yet come of age. The majority of its members have yet to reach the full level of rational consciousness that would enable them to resolve conflicts by negotiation, compromise, forgiveness, and mutual respect. The intuitive level of con-sciousness is a further development beyond even that marvelous evolutionary accomplishment.

The Human Condition and the Resurrection

When we look at the colossal tragedy of September 11, we can see how deeply our human family needs to be called out of its lethargy and indifference, its acceptance of evil and violence, and its toleration of the inequalities that exist throughout the world. Through such an understanding, we may have a chance of solving the mammoth world problems of our time at their roots and not just with patchwork efforts or, however helpful it might be at times, with money alone.

A change of attitude and consciousness enables us to feel the sufferings and needs of others as our own. It allows us to feel that it was not just those particular people who died in the Twin Towers attack: something in us also died there. The events of September 11 have undermined our dependency on support systems that kept in place our rigid ideas of who we are or want to become. Through this immense catastrophe as well as others yet to happen, God may bring about for future generations a quality of life that is far beyond anything we can imagine.

Suffering is never an end in itself, but a stepping stone to transformation. In this view it may be a necessary step to force us to let go of what we overly depend on for the fulfillment of our idea of happiness. And if we die in the process, we will be contributing to the transformation of the human family, just as those people did who died in the Twin Towers.

All that the victims of the attack were thinking about at the end were their families and how to say goodbye. To escape the flames, some of them had to jump out of the windows. What I saw was Christ in those people, enduring his passion once again. They could say with St. Paul, "I bear for your sake…what is lacking to the sufferings of Christ" (Colossians 1:24).

Thus, while there may be other tragedies, and terrorist attacks, the events of September 11 are not going to destroy God's plan for the inner transformation of the human race.

The Oneness of the Human Family

The oneness of the human family that is presupposed in Christ's passion, death, and resurrection deserves more elaboration. There are three stages in Christ's passion in which he identifies with the human condition at its deep level of individual and social weakness and alienation.

The first stage is when Christ was asked by God the Father in his agony in the Garden of Gethsemane to take into his own consciousness the psychological and spiritual consequences of our feelings of alienation—from other people, from God, or from ourselves. This suffering can be so overwhelming that it leads to mental and physical illness.

Jesus did not die for a few misdemeanors. He experienced the psychological consequences of our going against our conscience in major decisions in our lives: such feelings as an inner sense of alienation, loneliness, desolation, and utter powerlessness. These are the kinds of suffering that people experience in the Night of the Spirit as part of the unfolding of the spiritual journey. But they are also the pain and horror that constitute the state of separation from God caused by sin. And this is precisely what Paul refers to when he writes, "For our sakes God made sin of him who knew no sin, so that in him we might become God's holiness" (II Corinthians 5:21).

We hear the desperate plea of Jesus during his agony in the Garden of Gethsemane, "Father, if it be possible, let this cup pass from me" (Mark 14:36). Jesus felt the fullness of human destitution and spiritual poverty in that cup. To drink that cup was to taste the desolation that the greatest of sinners and violators of human rights have ever felt. In other words, to be a sinner in that sense is to be the opposite of God, or to feel abandoned by God— even rejected by God. It is those precise feelings that were present in that cup. Therefore, Jesus' cry to let the cup pass from him really means, "I can't drink it. I'm dying from this unbearable anguish. Father, if it be possible, take it away." This is the cry of human weakness reaching to infinity. It express- es Jesus' complete identification with the burdened conscience of every person who has ever lived or will ever live.

The response of Jesus to his agony is contained in the second part of his prayer: "Nevertheless, not my will but thine be done!" (Mark 14:36). This is the cry of divine love reaching to infinity. "Yes," the cry was saying, "I will take into myself the suffering of every individual together with the collective suf- fering of all humanity."

As Christians, we believe that in baptism we are incorporated into the mystical body of Christ, and become cells in his glorified body (I Corinthians 12:12–27). The same Spirit and dispositions that are in Christ are present in us, inspiring us with the same willingness to open ourselves to everybody's sufferings, insofar as we are capable of bearing them. Moreover, we are not just individuals. We are individual *and* social in our very being. We cannot be individuals without being totally united with everybody else, and we cannot be united with everybody else without being an individual member of the mystical body of Christ.

Biology teaches that each cell works for the good of the whole organism, independently of its own good. It follows the instructions of the DNA encoded within every one of our cells. In a similar way, we might say that the Spirit of Christ has been poured into us. The divine DNA bestows on each of us the whole program for human transformation. The ultimate Christian project is to enable the unfolding of the divine DNA into the fullness of transformation in Christ. And this unfolding is not just for us. The project to which God has invited us in the gospel is not only the transformation of the individual, but a participation in and contribution to the transformation of the whole of humanity.

Jesus' saying, "What you did to the least of these little ones, you did to me" (Matthew 25:40) implies that he is present in everyone else. Similarly, this acknowledgment could only happen if there is at the deepest level of human nature a oneness that underlies every one of us as individuals and in some degree penetrates our consciousness. More and more, as we mature as human beings and in the deep knowledge of God, we are being brought into

the divine presence. According to Saint John of the
Cross, our overall degree of wellness as a person
depends on our conscious relationship with God.[1]
To whatever degree grace has not been fully realized in us, we suffer some degree of illness.

The second moment of Christ's descent into
the human condition is on the cross, where he says,
"My God, my God, why have you forsaken me?"
(Matthew 27:46). The word Jesus normally uses for
God the Father is "Abba," which in Aramaic was an
endearing and intimate word that can be translated
roughly as "Daddy." This text suggests that on the
cross Christ's psychological sense of his identity as
the Son of God was obscured. And in a sense it
would have to be. If he was to become sin, he
would have to feel the full weight of total separation from the God who up to that moment had
been everything to him. In this sense, Christ let go
of his identity as the Son of God in order to iden-
tify with every human being—past, present, and to
come—all of whom are in need of redemption and
destined for divine transformation.

The third and final moment, one that is high-
lighted in the Eastern Orthodox liturgy of Holy
Saturday, is the teaching that Jesus descended into

hell after his death. There are several different opin-
ions as to what this descent could really mean. In
any case, in the Apostles' Creed it is stated: "He suf-
fered under Pontius Pilate, was crucified, died, and
was buried. He descended into hell." In some way,
God dies in the death of Jesus. The descent of Jesus
into hell is the sign that God joins us in every kind
of suffering, even in the suffering that is the natural
consequence of personal sin.

Perhaps we might affirm that it is not so much
personal sin that hurts God, but the pain that we
feel as the consequence of our sins. When we accept
that pain, God comes to heal us and to unite us to
himself—a place at the very depths of our suffering.
In his descent into hell Jesus has taken the whole of
human moral evil into himself in order to plunge it
into the abyss of God's infinite mercy and thus to
take it away.

The Sins of the World

If Christ has taken away the sins of the world,
where, we may ask, are they? The answer is that they
are nowhere. As soon as we turn to Christ, our sins
are destroyed. As Paul puts it, "Jesus died for our sins
and rose for our justification" (Romans 4:25), a

short formula that puts in a nutshell the totality of Christ's love for us, which in turn manifests the infinite love of the Father for us.

In this way, we can see that the passion of Jesus and the myriad forms of violence that are now creating a vast ocean of human suffering—one that we are aware of more and more insistently through the mass media—are not total disasters, but may actually be the seeds of resurrection. As Paul teaches, nothing can separate us from the love of Christ— neither death nor anything else. This attitude in the face of the present crisis can help us to measure the kind of defensive activity that we take. It must not be excessive, or done for motives of retaliation, revenge, or the desire for a vindictive triumph.

The fact that terrorists think and act the way they do may be attributed in part to the failure of nations and governments to respond to the great needs of developing countries and of the poor in general. We are now confronted with a situation that has reached a point where we have *no* control, or at the least no *absolute* control, over our lives. In such situations, where do we place our confidence?

We need to pray that the oneness of the human family will become an invincible conviction, and that we may have the discernment to know how to respond to these uncertain times.

Christ's love for us is not sentimental. It is the most powerful force in the world. Paul prays that we may understand its length and height and breadth and depth (cf. Ephesians 3:14-19). It is this love that we access in contemplative prayer. At the same time, our prayer needs to manifest itself in the quality of our daily lives. One of the gifts we may think of giving to the human family at this point in its evolution is the effort to relate to other people's needs more profoundly than we have done before. We need to reach out to those who oppose us in reconciliation, patience, and compassion. We all suffer from the human condition and long to escape from our common misery. Why not hold hands and help each other climb out of the swamp rather than fight over the real estate?

There is a picture of the Twin Towers drawn by a child that appeared in the newspapers shortly after the attack. It was a picture of the two towers with arms reaching out to each other, and each pair of arms was trying to hold up the other tower. This picture comes from the heart of a child, but it certainly touches a very deep issue: in holding our arms up to God for the infinite mercy that is always available, we do not succeed in isolation. We need the help of each other.

Centering Prayer and Our Responsibilities to the World

Many are still suffering the fallout from the horrors of the attack on September 11. Those who are deeply committed to centering prayer may wish to lengthen their periods of prayer. It might be only five minutes; others may wish to add another session. This may mean that we will be more open to the values of the inner room that we enter during centering prayer, where we expose ourselves completely to the divine presence, and where, by virtue of sitting on the cross with Christ, so to speak, we renew our baptismal commitment to the death of the false self and the resurrection of the true self. This primary significance of baptism is also the primary value of contemplative prayer.

In this perspective, the very difficulties we have in the centering prayer practice and in the evolution of our spiritual journey are signs that we are sharing the passion of Christ. The whole human family joins us in our spiritual journey and benefits from our progress in God's love.

The present circumstances seem to be teaching us that we are accountable for everyone on earth—past, present, and to come. There is no way of separating our fate from the fate of others. This may mean that we share the fate of those who are suffering, or at the very least it means that we feel for those who do, and do what we can to manifest the goodness and tenderness of God through the practice of compassion for and genuine love of one another.

[1] From *America* March 22, 1997 in an article by Kevin Culligan.

I turn now to the consideration of practical ways of bringing assistance to others in everyday life and thus pouring the energy of God's immense love into the global environment. As a way of illustrating this disposition, let me explore the implications of the gospel story of the Wedding Feast of Cana in Galilee (John 2:1–11).

❈ *Part Two* ❈

The Wedding Feast of Cana

On the third day there was a wedding at Cana in Galilee, and the mother of Jesus was there. Jesus and his disciples had likewise been invited to the celebration. At a certain point the wine ran out, and Jesus' mother told him, "They have no more wine." Jesus replied, "Woman, how does this concern of yours involve me? My hour has not yet come."

His mother instructed those waiting on table, "Do whatever he tells you." As prescribed for Jewish ceremonial washings, there were at hand six stone water jugs, each one holding fifteen to twenty-five gallons. "Fill those jars with water," Jesus ordered, at which they filled them to the brim. "Now," he said, "draw some out and take it to the waiter in charge." They did as he instructed them.

The waiter in charge tasted the water made wine, without knowing where it had come from; only the waiters knew, since they had drawn the water. Then the waiter in charge called the groom over and remarked to him: "People usually serve the choice wine first; then when the guests have been drinking awhile, a lesser vintage. What you have done is keep the choice wine until now."

Jesus performed this first of his signs at Cana in Galilee. Thus, did he reveal his glory, and his disciples believed in him.

(John 2:1–11)

J OHN TELLS US that this is the first of Jesus' miracles. It has a special place in the Christmas-Epiphany liturgy where we are invited to celebrate the revelation of the divinity of Jesus in a series of historical events. On Christmas Day, we celebrate the appearance of the Word made flesh as the Babe of Bethlehem. The full significance of this appearance unfolds on the feast of the Epiphany, which means "manifestation" and is the crown of the Christmas mystery. On that feast, three different events are celebrated. These events, which are the coming of the Magi, the Baptism of Jesus in the River Jordan, and the wedding feast of Cana, have less to do with historical time than with the spiritual meaning of the historical events.

The Three Events
The coming of the Magi symbolizes the remote call of the whole human family to divine union. The Magi, or astrologers, came from the East. They symbolize seekers of the truth throughout the ages.

Looking at the story from the perspective of divine grace, the arrival of the Magi signifies the fact that all human beings, whoever they are and whenever they may be born, have an invitation to transformation into the divine nature insofar as that is possible for a human being.

The story alerts us that the Christian religion is not just about becoming a better person as such, but about being *divinized,* as the Greek fathers called it—sharers in the interior life of God, which is the eternal movement of infinite love between the Father, Son, and Holy Spirit within the Godhead.

The second event that is celebrated on the feast of the Epiphany is Christ's baptism at the River Jordan. The Spirit descends upon Jesus, and the voice of the Father proclaims, "This is my beloved Son. Listen to him" (Matthew 3.17). This event represents the manifestation of Christ Jesus to the people of Israel.

The marriage feast of Cana is celebrated a few days later in the Christian liturgical calendar. On this feast Jesus' divinity is manifested to his disciples.

There is a gradation here. First, there is the remote call of everyone to divine union in the persons of the Magi. At Jesus' baptism in the Jordan there occurs a proximate invitation. Finally, the wedding feast of Cana symbolizes the celebration of the unity between the divine-human person of Christ and each of us. It is also the marriage of God with each of us. We do not earn this invitation, but we do have to accept it in order to consummate our union with God. Nor are we asked merely to celebrate it as a guest, but to be assimilated by it, and to fully enjoy it.

This is what Jesus means by eternal life, which is not so much a place as a state of consciousness or, more precisely, Christ's consciousness of the Father as he understood him.

Mary's Statement

In the course of the marriage feast at Cana, Jesus seems to be trying to discern whether it is time for him to manifest his divine person to the disciples. Perhaps Jesus had in mind a special time to do it, maybe on a retreat or in some sort of private setting. Let us recall that the Spirit operates in us today in the same way the Spirit worked with Jesus' disciples and friends.

Keeping that background in mind, this incident assumes great significance. Apparently, two acquaintances of Mary have just been married. Jesus and some of his disciples have been invited to the banquet. At some point, the wine is running out. For young spouses, this is a source of great distress. The couple is in danger of being embarrassed because they have not prepared adequately for the refreshment of the guests; Mary, it appears, does not want this to happen. Accordingly, she says to Jesus, "They have no more wine."

This is not exactly a request, yet, in a way, Mary's statement is the most profound and powerful kind of request. She does not ask anything of Jesus. Rather, she simply states the problem. She leaves the decision to him. Mary manifests a delicate concern for a fairly insignificant problem as we would think of it; but it was a problem for these two newlyweds, just starting life together and trying to make a good impression on their friends and relatives.

Mary's statement of concern puts Jesus in a difficult situation. He hears what she is saying, but he is not sure that it is the right time to act in a way that would reveal his divinity to his disciples. After all, his disciples at this time were a pretty thick-headed bunch, and it took them a long time to learn anything. To anticipate such a major revelation, he needed to find out in what spirit an act is being suggested that he knew would have great significance and indeed eternal consequences.

This is why, when Mary remarks, "They have no more wine," Jesus wants to know where her concern is coming from. Is this, he wonders, simply an ordinary concern that his mother has for these young acquaintances of hers, or could it be a movement of the Holy Spirit that aims to transform Mary's casual remark into a major revelation of Christ's divinity to the disciples, who are to pass on his teaching and example to posterity? It is a crucial issue for him. In the present translation of the text the response is somewhat obscure. But the message is clear. According to the text that we read in the liturgy, Jesus says, "How does this concern of yours involve me?" In other words, "I recognize your concern, and I sympathize with it, but why do you want me to get involved?"

By asking that question, Jesus invites Mary to clarify whether she wants him to solve the problem or is willing to let the matter drop. Notice that Mary does not put any pressure on him. The event is a marvelous example of how to ask God for things. It is better to leave the response to our requests up to God: simply lay out the problem, and then let God decide what to do, rather than plead with or cajole him into doing what we want. Detachment from our own desires makes the petition all the more powerful. The situation will always be answered, but not necessarily in the way that we want or expected.

Do Whatever He Tells You

At this point, the Blessed Mother turns to the wait-ers, saying, "Do whatever he tells you." In saying this, she gives Jesus the maximum freedom to do whatever he likes. He can tell the waiters, "Do noth-ing," or he can tell them to do something, which is what he actually does: "Fill the six jars that are sit-ting there with water."

I suppose Jesus could also have provided the wine in another way. He didn't necessarily have to work a miracle. For example, he could have sent the disciples to buy more wine at a shop downtown. In any case, he realized that the issue was whether or not to work a miracle that would transform the hearts of his disciples. Thus the disciples would become faith-filled students ready to be trained as apostles of the Word of God.

Let us continue with the story.

Mary said to the waiters, "Do whatever he tells you." This is a good piece of advice for any occasion. In this case, Jesus summons the waiters and tells them to fill the six empty jars with water. Six is the number of creation in Jewish numerology, since in six days, according to the Book of Genesis, the uni-verse was created.

For those familiar with that symbology, the six jars represent not only the first creation, but also the previous covenants between God and Israel: the Abrahamic covenant and the covenant with Moses on Mount Sinai. They stand for the revelation of God that was originally offered to the Jewish people, and which they, as best they could, faithfully fulfilled by bringing the knowledge of the one true God into human history.

When the six jars are filled with water, and Jesus says to the waiters, "Take some to the headwaiter and see what he thinks of it." The six jars contain some twenty-five gallons each. That is a *lot* of wine, even for a wedding—enough for a small army. The waiters take a portion of the contents of one of the jars to the headwaiter. He has no idea where the wine has come from. The headwaiter is so impressed that he immediately calls the groom over, and makes this little quip: "Most people serve the good wine first, and then when everyone has been drinking for a while, they then serve the less good. But you have saved the best wine until now!" It is a charming compliment that must have made the young bridegroom feel very happy.

However, the compliment has cosmic ramifications. The water transformed into wine symbolizes the overflowing infusion of the Holy Spirit that will occur at Pentecost as a result of Christ's passion, death, and resurrection. The wine, with its heady, exuberant, and inebriating quality and delicious taste, symbolically replaces the Old Law with its strict rules.

In this way, we can see that the very objects that Jesus uses to manifest the changing of water into wine are providing us with a whole theology of the New Testament. The New Covenant, as he calls it, is a transmission of the divine nature by means of which human nature is not merely improved but made new, changed in a way that produces a new creation. The wine represents the spirit of the gospel that Christ is bringing into the world and that he intends to communicate with the help of his disciples.

As Jesus indicates in another place, new wine has to be put into new wineskins (Matthew 9:17). The old structures will not work. The Spirit does not like to be confined in a jar or a box, but is constantly bursting out of all kinds of human limitations to bring the love of God and the energy of divine life into the world. As Jesus says in another place, "I have come to throw a firebrand upon the earth—that is my mission! And oh, how I wish it were already in a blaze" (Luke 12:49).

Thus the wedding feast suddenly changes from being a homey concern that Mary had for her recently married friends into an extraordinary revelation of the Christian dispensation. Notice the final sentence: "Jesus revealed his glory." This is to say that Jesus revealed the divinity dwelling in himself (this is what "glory" normally means in the New Testament) "and his disciples believed in him."

The Ordinary Becomes Extraordinary

It would be hard to imagine a moment full of greater significance than this, yet it is an ordinary social event that sets it off. Just as ordinary life is filled with casual remarks and little concerns, it is precisely these very trivialities that God sometimes uses to communicate with us or to initiate some significant movement of grace for the healing of a family, a community, or the world.

Many of the religious orders, for instance, came into being by that kind of chance. Some good-hearted soul noticed a group of people with a special need—the poor, the sick, orphans, or some other group in straitened circumstances—and decided to do something about it. Most founders did not have the grandiose idea of instituting a religious order. They simply did what seemed to be appropriate at the time. In this case, what they did was actually inspired by the Spirit.

Sometimes a joke is only a joke. At other times, as in the case of the headwaiter, God uses the joke as a word of wisdom that sets in motion the action of grace that goes far beyond what the occasion might warrant, or that anyone suspects.

To return to the theme of what occurred on September 11, the wedding feast at Cana suggests that while nobody is asking all of us to go to Afghanistan and shoot terrorists, there may be someone down the street or in our family for whom we could show concern. It is the raising of the quality of one's life, something that Mary exemplifies in this particular case, that is an occasion for God to pour compassion, forgiveness, and reconciliation into a troubled situation.

One of the things each of us can do to contribute to the peace of the world right now is to think of how we could bring more kindness and concern into our daily activities, however trivial. If your husband is constantly burning his fingers on the old coffeepot, you might think of buying a new one. Or, if you notice how somebody is finding it hard to get to an event, you might arrange some kind of transportation. These are trivial, everyday things, but this is exactly where the kingdom of God is normally at work, at least in Jesus' teaching. The kingdom of God is not only in sacred places, nor does it operate mainly on sacred feast days— although these may sometimes be contributory factors. What the kingdom of God points to is the fact that daily life in its ordinary routines is the place where the kingdom is most active and where anybody can do something of great value. Like Mary's tiny act of concern, a simple loving concern can be turned into a cosmic event by the power of the Spirit.

There are basically only two things needed for transformation: suffering and love. Everybody has this capacity. Hence, everybody is a possible subject for divine transformation.

God does not do everything by himself. Instead, he prefers to operate through us. As human beings, we have a certain intelligence, and every now and again God thinks it is time for us to use these faculties and do something for the benefit of those around us. But that act does not have to be grandiose or sensational. It can be something within easy reach.

The Contemplative Life

Everybody who does centering prayer always asks, "How can I be a contemplative in everyday life, with its noise, turmoil, and constant interruptions? How can I be interiorly quiet when the world is getting noisier and the pace of life faster?"

The answer is to slow down and pray more. Prayer has the great advantage of giving us a perspective on what we have to do. If we practice contemplative prayer every day, we find that we have more time for everything else. This is because we were doing a lot of things that we don't really have to do. Contemplative prayer cultivates the gift of discernment. Spiritual discernment is not something we have to try to do; it arises spontaneously as one of the fruits of the Spirit communicated to us during contemplative prayer.

The greatest source of security, independence, and true love is the firm conviction that the Divine Trinity—Father, Son, and Holy Spirit—dwells within us all the time, twenty-four hours a day, under all circumstances, and is totally available to us.

In every circumstance, however tragic or horrendous, difficult or trivial, this presence is always there. That means that the Spirit is counseling us in what to do in difficult situations, and that the Father is always present, holding us in an embrace of infinite tenderness and empowering us to manifest his presence in every moment. The chief job of a Christian is to manifest divine love in everything we do. The Spirit patiently guides us step by step through our whole lives in the course of our spiritual journey, inviting us to look at what was good in our life and to reinforce it, and to allow what was not so good to be put on the junk pile. As God works back through our personal history, he comes to early childhood, where most of the problems actually began. These problems we have either repressed into the unconscious or developed compensatory activities to deal with.

But as the Spirit brings us closer to the source of our difficulties, and as we become aware of specific traumatic experiences—such as rejection, abandonment, loss of a parent, persecution by peers, disappointments, failures—it can seem to us that we are getting worse. Of course, we are not really getting worse. We are just finding out how badly off we always were. The purpose of this process is to see how we can free ourselves from childish influences that stick to us like molasses on a piece of clothing. Therefore, our spiritual practice is to work with God dwelling within us, with incredible closeness, tenderness, and love. God never punishes us in this process of purification. In fact, God is only concerned for our healing. His will is to communicate the maximum amount of divine love that we can possibly receive. And if we fill that up, God enlarges our capacity so we can receive still more. God is not interested in judgment for or against anyone, but in

communicating the gift of his own being to everyone.

When we look at the cross, we are really looking at God the Father giving himself away to us in
the person of his greatest treasure, namely, his Son. It
is as if the Father is saying: "I'm giving you my Son
as the proof of how much I want to give myself to
you and to bring you into the fullest possible share
in my divine life."

God the Grandparent

I do not believe the world will be damaged by over-
rating God's love for us. The problem has been that
most of us are for some reason too hesitant. I agree
that God can be a little intimidating because of the
largeness of his presence. But by spending time in his
company, we begin to see that our life is surround-
ed by this immense intelligence, who figures out all
kinds of ways of getting around our faults and sins
and making good things happen to us, even when
we are making mistakes at almost every step.

All our stumblings don't cause God distress or
annoyance, but probably a great deal of amusement
and pleasure. Just as a grandparent enjoys holding his
or her grandchild, so does God enjoy holding us in
his arms. And they are not asking the child to say or
do anything. They are just thrilled to hold this little

creature that is so special in their eyes. And if the child opens its eyes or simply smiles, grandparents are in ecstasy for several days. God holds us in being at every moment. Otherwise, we would just disappear or turn into a grease spot. We don't have to earn God's love. It is hard enough just to receive it, given the human condition.

God is not necessarily going to take away all our difficulties. He does something much more wonderful, which is to join us in them. Thus they become redeeming and healing for ourselves, and at the same time a means of healing for everyone we love, and indeed for everyone in the whole world.

In the parable of the Prodigal Son, both sons treated their father outrageously—one by living the good life and making a mess of it, and the other by behaving well, chiefly for the sake of receiving the inheritance. Yet the father never complained or even reprimanded either of them. What was the bottom line? He only asked them to live together in peace, because he loved them both so much.

If you want to give God pleasure, trying to live in peace with everyone is a sure way of doing so. There is nothing to be afraid of in the present world situation. It may look like a disaster if you get injured or hurt; and it is. Nevertheless, such injury is not the ultimate disaster. For in God's goodness, everything that happens to us has the capacity to raise us up through an inner resurrection that enables us to see every tragedy, mistake, and even sin as part of God's plan for our healing.

Nothing can describe how deep God's love is. In him, with him, and through him we will have the strength to see beyond every tragedy that may lie ahead of us. Whatever happens, since God is present in us, nothing can disturb the basic peace that is there, the peace that Paul says "surpasses all under-standing." The divine presence empowers us to per-ceive what God is asking us to do in each circum-stance as it unfolds, without being anxious or fear-ful. Fear, as Jesus said, is useless. The "fear of God" in scripture is a technical term that means being con-tinuously attentive to the presence of God. When that loving presence is experienced within, we see it in everyone else.

❈

green press
INITIATIVE

Lantern Books has elected to print this title on Rolland Enviro a 100% post-consumer recycled paper, processed chlorine-free. As a result, we have saved the following resources:

3 Trees (40' tall and 6-8" diameter)
914 Gallons of Wastewater
2 million BTU's of Total Energy
117 Pounds of Solid Waste
220 Pounds of Greenhouse Gases

As part of Lantern Books' commitment to the environment we have joined the Green Press Initiative, a nonprofit organization supporting publishers in using fiber that is not sourced from ancient or endangered forests. We hope that you, the reader, will support Lantern and the Green Press Initiative in our endeavor to preserve the ancient forests and the natural systems on which all life depends. One way is to buy books that cost a little more but make a positive commitment to the environment not only in their words, but in the paper that they were published on. For more information, visit www.greenpressinitiative.org

Environmental impact estimates were made using the Environmental Defense Paper Calculator. For more information visit: www.papercalculator.org.

LANTERN BOOKS WRITTEN BY
OR FEATURING THOMAS KEATING

The Divine Indwelling: Centering Prayer and Its Development (2001), $10.00 pbk

Fruits and Gifts of the Spirit (2000), $12.00 pbk

St. Thérèse of Lisieux: A Transformation in Christ (2000), $10.00 pbk

Sundays at the Magic Monastery: Homilies from the Trappists of St. Benedict's Monastery (2002), $15.00 pbk